Place Value Lessons for Kids

Math 2nd Grade
Children's Math Books

Hi there! What's up?

Let's learn about Place Value.

Are you Ready?
Okay, let's start!

This is a Place Value House. As you can see there are three rooms in it, the hundreds, tens and ones. Each room will only allow 1 digit, so if you have number 152, this is how you place it (see below).

Based on the example on left page.
Let us integrate it with blocks.

 = 100    = 10   ⬜ = 1

1   5   2

Hundreds	Tens	Ones

100 blocks   **50** blocks   **2** blocks

This is how you say it:

One hundred and fifty-two **blocks**

One last example:

28

· ·

2 **8**

| Hundreds | Tens | Ones |

20 blocks **8** blocks

This is how you say it:

Twenty-eight blocks

Okay! It's time to practice what you have learned.

Have fun learning with these cool Place Value activities!

Enjoy!

BUILD A 2-3 DIGITS NUMBER FROM THE PARTS

Warm up with writing 2-3 digit numbers.

Example:

$$\underline{\hspace{2cm}} \quad 30 + 9$$

Answer: 39

Write your answer on the blank.

$$\underline{\quad 39 \quad} \quad 30 + 9$$

BUILD A 2-DIGITS NUMBER FROM THE PARTS

Write the 2 digit numbers.

1. __________ 50 + 2

2. __________ 70 + 3

3. __________ 60 + 5

4. __________ 70 + 0

5. __________ 70 + 4

6. __________ 70 + 3

7. __________ 30 + 7

BUILD A 2-DIGITS NUMBER FROM THE PARTS

Write the 2 digit numbers.

1. _____________ 60 + 6

2. _____________ 30 + 5

3. _____________ 90 + 0

4. _____________ 10 + 4

5. _____________ 90 + 3

6. _____________ 40 + 2

7. _____________ 60 + 0

BUILD A 2-DIGITS NUMBER FROM THE PARTS

Write the 2 digit numbers.

1. __________   10 + 3

2. __________   20 + 1

3. __________   50 + 7

4. __________   50 + 3

5. __________   80 + 9

6. __________   70 + 6

7. __________   20 + 9

BUILD A 2-DIGITS NUMBER FROM THE PARTS

Write the 2 digit numbers.

1. __________ 30 + 4

2. __________ 40 + 5

3. __________ 20 + 4

4. __________ 10 + 8

5. __________ 10 + 6

6. __________ 60 + 5

7. __________ 50 + 6

BUILD A 2-DIGITS NUMBER FROM THE PARTS

Write the 2 digit numbers.

1. _____________ 70 + 4

2. _____________ 90 + 0

3. _____________ 30 + 2

4. _____________ 40 + 7

5. _____________ 50 + 6

6. _____________ 50 + 4

7. _____________ 80 + 4

BUILD A 2-DIGITS NUMBER FROM THE PARTS

Write the 2 digit numbers.

1. __________   40 + 8

2. __________   70 + 1

3. __________   40 + 1

4. __________   60 + 1

5. __________   50 + 3

6. __________   30 + 8

7. __________   90 + 6

BUILD A 2-DIGITS NUMBER FROM THE PARTS

Write the 2 digit numbers.

1. __________ 20 + 2

2. __________ 80 + 6

3. __________ 80 + 3

4. __________ 20 + 9

5. __________ 20 + 0

6. __________ 40 + 1

7. __________ 40 + 2

BUILD A 2-DIGITS NUMBER FROM THE PARTS

Write the 2 digit numbers.

1. __________ 80 + 2

2. __________ 20 + 1

3. __________ 70 + 1

4. __________ 10 + 1

5. __________ 20 + 0

6. __________ 70 + 0

7. __________ 70 + 7

BUILD A 2-DIGITS NUMBER FROM THE PARTS

Write the 2 digit numbers.

1. __________ 30 + 5

2. __________ 50 + 5

3. __________ 40 + 4

4. __________ 50 + 3

5. __________ 40 + 7

6. __________ 80 + 5

7. __________ 80 + 3

BUILD A 2-DIGITS NUMBER FROM THE PARTS

Write the 2 digit numbers.

1. __________   10 + 6

2. __________   30 + 2

3. __________   40 + 7

4. __________   70 + 5

5. __________   10 + 6

6. __________   40 + 6

7. __________   70 + 5

BUILD A 3-DIGITS NUMBER FROM THE PARTS

Write the 3 digit numbers.

1. __________   700 + 50 + 1

2. __________   900 + 40 + 7

3. __________   300 + 40 + 9

4. __________   400 + 60 + 5

5. __________   500 + 80 + 5

6. __________   800 + 20 + 1

7. __________   300 + 10 + 0

BUILD A 3-DIGITS NUMBER FROM THE PARTS

Write the 3 digit numbers.

1. __________ 500 + 80 + 3

2. __________ 300 + 30 + 6

3. __________ 200 + 80 + 7

4. __________ 200 + 60 + 5

5. __________ 500 + 70 + 0

6. __________ 400 + 50 + 9

7. __________ 700 + 10 + 1

BUILD A 3-DIGITS NUMBER FROM THE PARTS

Write the 3 digit numbers.

1. ______________ 400 + 40 + 3

2. ______________ 100 + 70 + 1

3. ______________ 900 + 80 + 4

4. ______________ 200 + 90 + 2

5. ______________ 600 + 90 + 0

6. ______________ 300 + 50 + 2

7. ______________ 700 + 80 + 5

Write the 3 digit numbers.

1. _____________ 500 + 70 + 4

2. _____________ 600 + 60 + 1

3. _____________ 600 + 70 + 6

4. _____________ 600 + 50 + 3

5. _____________ 300 + 60 + 5

6. _____________ 900 + 80 + 4

7. _____________ 900 + 30 + 9

BUILD A 3-DIGITS NUMBER FROM THE PARTS

Write the 3 digit numbers.

1. __________   500 + 40 + 2

2. __________   800 + 60 + 4

3. __________   800 + 20 + 1

4. __________   500 + 10 + 0

5. __________   600 + 80 + 1

6. __________   500 + 50 + 4

7. __________   100 + 10 + 4

BUILD A 3-DIGITS NUMBER FROM THE PARTS

Write the 3 digit numbers.

1. __________ 200 + 90 + 1

2. __________ 700 + 10 + 3

3. __________ 900 + 60 + 5

4. __________ 500 + 50 + 4

5. __________ 900 + 20 + 6

6. __________ 200 + 30 + 6

7. __________ 800 + 60 + 0

BUILD A 3-DIGITS NUMBER FROM THE PARTS

Write the 3 digit numbers.

1. __________ 800 + 80 + 4

2. __________ 200 + 70 + 1

3. __________ 700 + 30 + 8

4. __________ 500 + 90 + 0

5. __________ 200 + 70 + 0

6. __________ 400 + 40 + 3

7. __________ 100 + 20 + 9

BUILD A 3-DIGITS NUMBER FROM THE PARTS

Write the 3 digit numbers.

1. _____________ 600 + 80 + 1

2. _____________ 900 + 40 + 6

3. _____________ 400 + 60 + 9

4. _____________ 700 + 10 + 3

5. _____________ 200 + 20 + 2

6. _____________ 600 + 60 + 6

7. _____________ 900 + 20 + 1

BUILD A 3-DIGITS NUMBER FROM THE PARTS

Write the 3 digit numbers.

1. _______________ 400 + 10 + 2

2. _______________ 200 + 70 + 2

3. _______________ 400 + 10 + 7

4. _______________ 500 + 40 + 0

5. _______________ 600 + 50 + 7

6. _______________ 500 + 90 + 9

7. _______________ 100 + 20 + 4

BUILD A 3-DIGITS NUMBER FROM THE PARTS

Write the 3 digit numbers.

1. __________ 600 + 40 + 4

2. __________ 400 + 70 + 1

3. __________ 400 + 70 + 7

4. __________ 300 + 90 + 9

5. __________ 400 + 20 + 5

6. __________ 100 + 60 + 2

7. __________ 500 + 40 + 4

FINDING THE PLACE VALUE

Find the value of each group of base ten blocks.

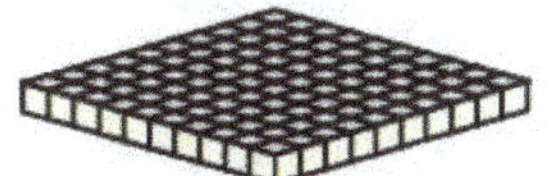 = 100   = 10   = 1

Write your answer on the blank.

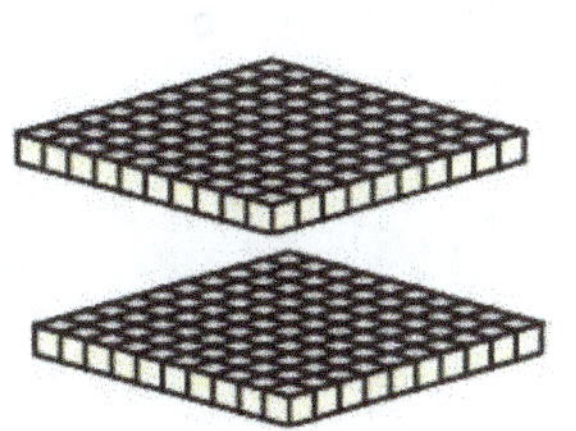 **2**
hundreds

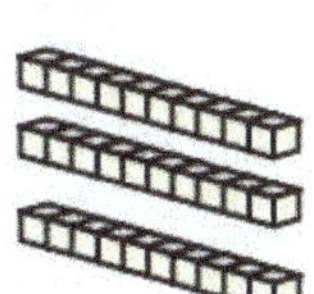 **3**
tens

1
ones

231
total

FINDING THE PLACE VALUE

Write your answers on the blank.

1.

_______ Hundreds   _______ Tens   _______ Ones

_______ Total

2.

_______ Hundreds   _______ Tens   _______ Ones

_______ Total

Write your answers on the blank.

1.

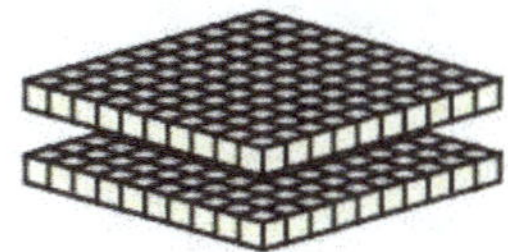 __________ Hundreds

 __________ Tens

__________ Ones

__________ Total

2.

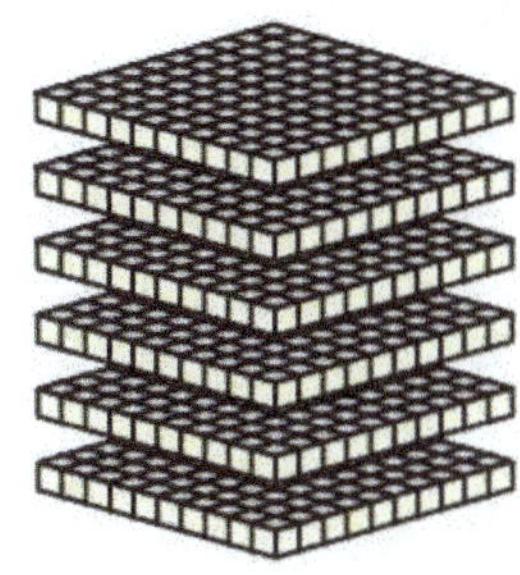 __________ Hundreds

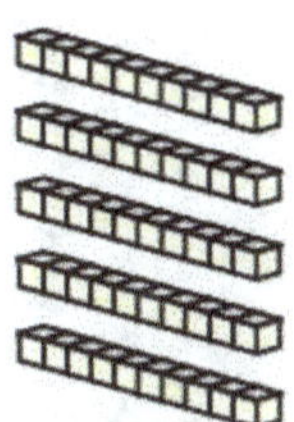 __________ Tens

__________ Ones

__________ Total

Write your answers on the blank.

1.

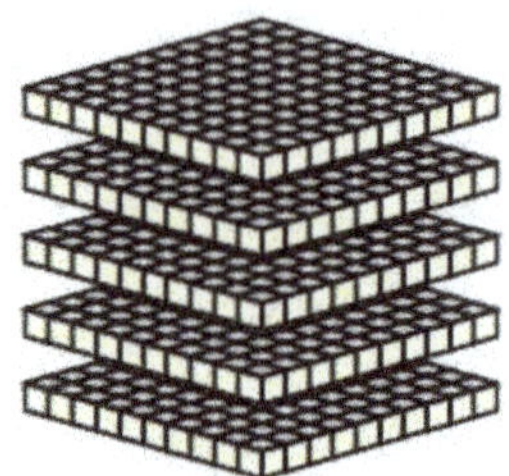 __________ Hundreds

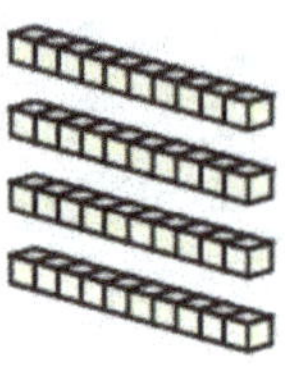 __________ Tens

 __________ Ones

__________ Total

2.

 __________ Hundreds

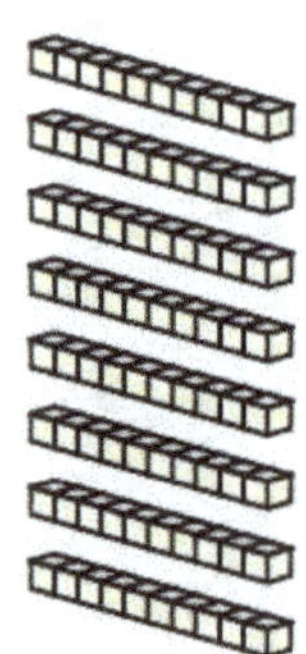 __________ Tens

__________ Ones

__________ Total

FINDING THE PLACE VALUE

Write your answers on the blank.

1.  _________ Hundreds   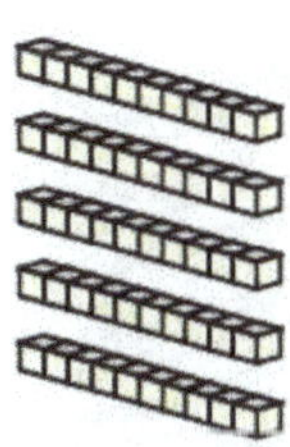 _________ Tens   _________ Ones

_________ Total

2.  _________ Hundreds   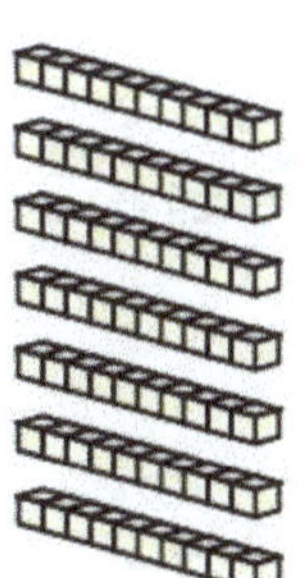 _________ Tens   _________ Ones

_________ Total

FINDING THE PLACE VALUE

Write your answers on the blank.

1.

__________ Hundreds   __________ Tens   __________ Ones

__________ Total

2.

__________ Hundreds   __________ Tens   __________ Ones

__________ Total

FINDING THE PLACE VALUE

Write your answers on the blank.

1. 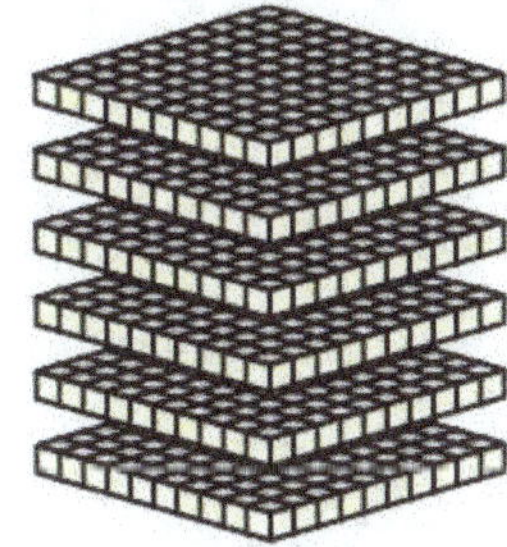 ________ Hundreds 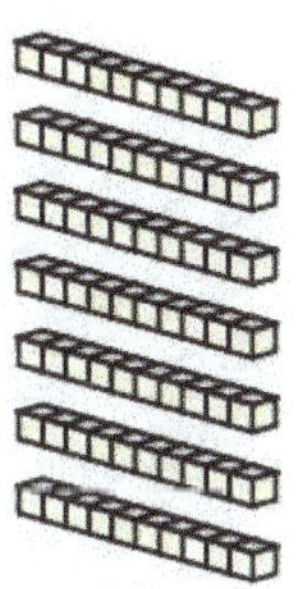 ________ Tens ________ Ones

________ Total

2.  ________ Hundreds 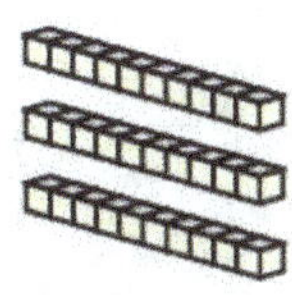 ________ Tens ________ Ones

________ Total

FINDING THE PLACE VALUE

Write your answers on the blank.

1.

 _______ Hundreds   _______ Tens   _______ Ones

_______ Total

2.

 _______ Hundreds   _______ Tens   _______ Ones

_______ Total

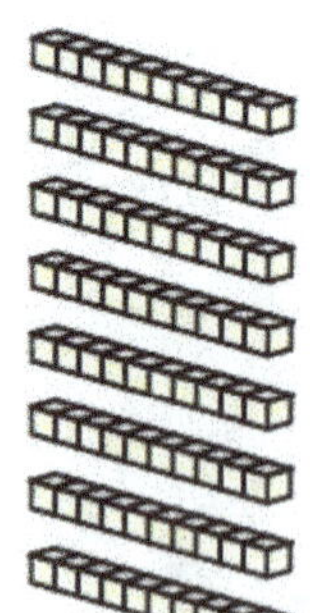

FINDING THE PLACE VALUE

Write your answers on the blank.

1.

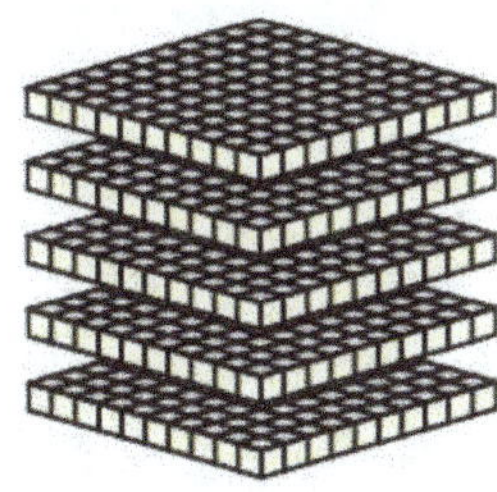 __________ Hundreds

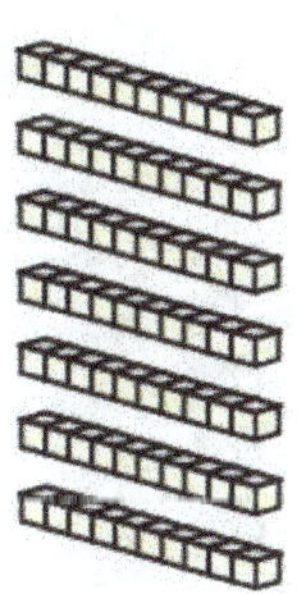 __________ Tens

__________ Ones

__________ Total

2.

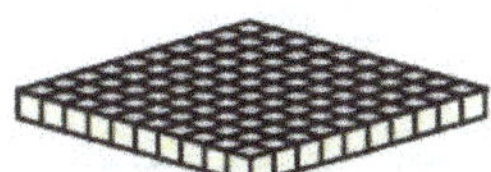 __________ Hundreds

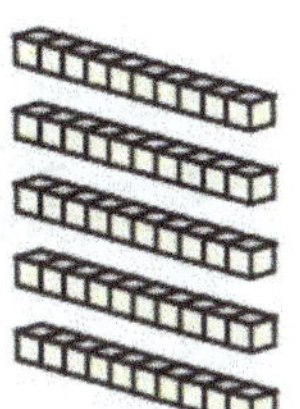 __________ Tens

__________ Ones

__________ Total

FINDING THE PLACE VALUE

Write your answers on the blank.

1.  __________ Hundreds   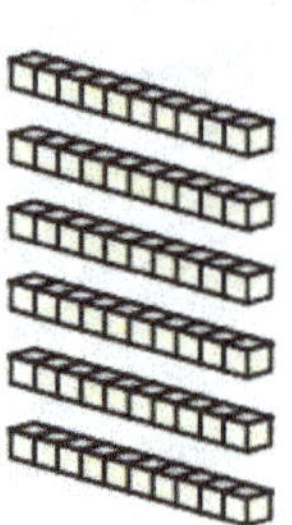 __________ Tens    __________ Ones

__________ Total

2. 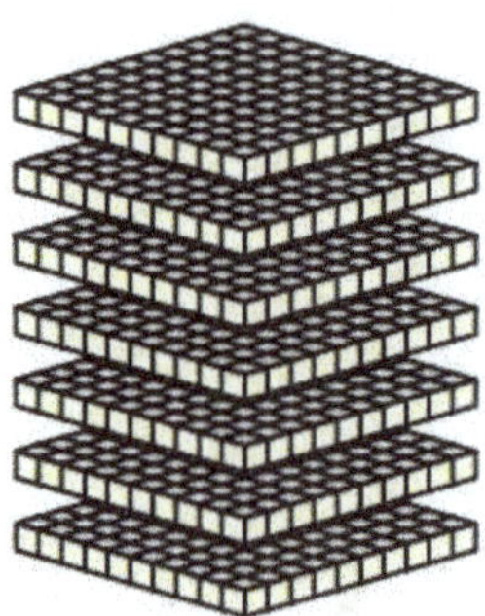 __________ Hundreds    __________ Tens   __________ Ones

__________ Total

Write your answers on the blank.

1.

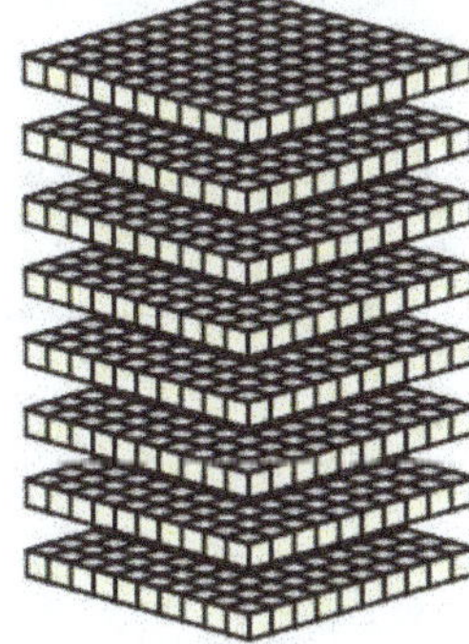 __________ Hundreds

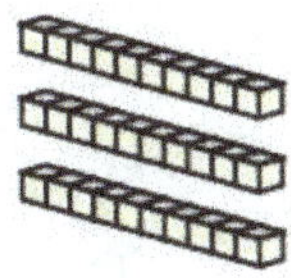 __________ Tens

__________ Ones

__________ Total

2.

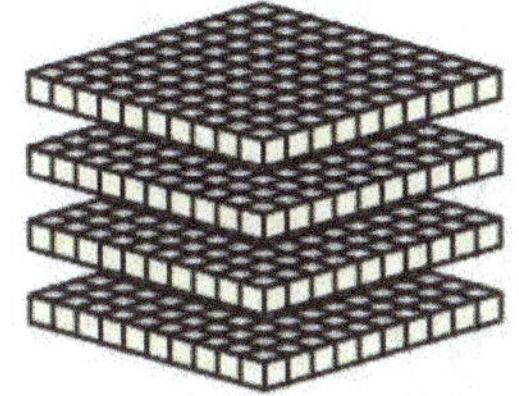 __________ Hundreds

__________ Tens

__________ Ones

__________ Total

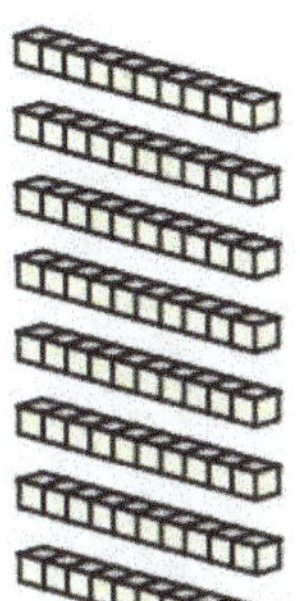

FINDING THE PLACE VALUE

Write your answers on the blank.

1.

 _______ Hundreds

 _______ Tens

_______ Ones

_______ Total

2.

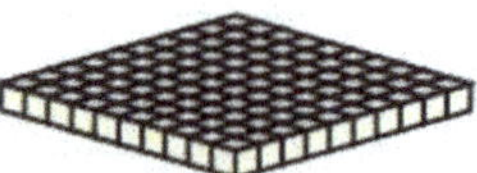 _______ Hundreds

 _______ Tens

_______ Ones

_______ Total

Write your answers on the blank.

1.
 __________ Hundreds

__________ Tens

__________ Ones

__________ Total

2.
 __________ Hundreds

__________ Tens

__________ Ones

__________ Total

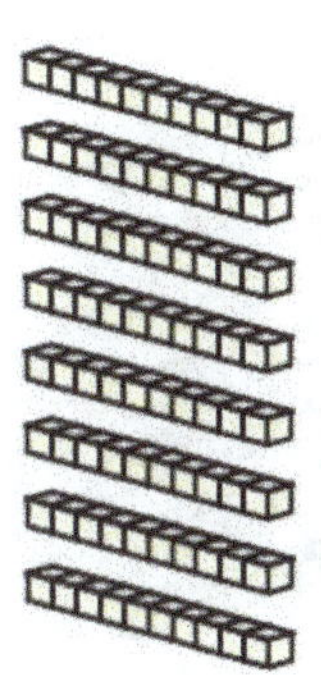

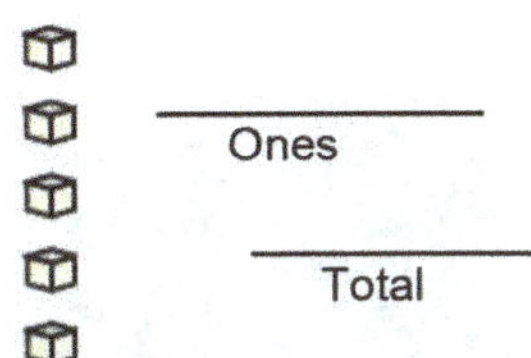

FINDING THE PLACE VALUE

ACTIVITY NO.
13

Write your answers on the blank.

1. 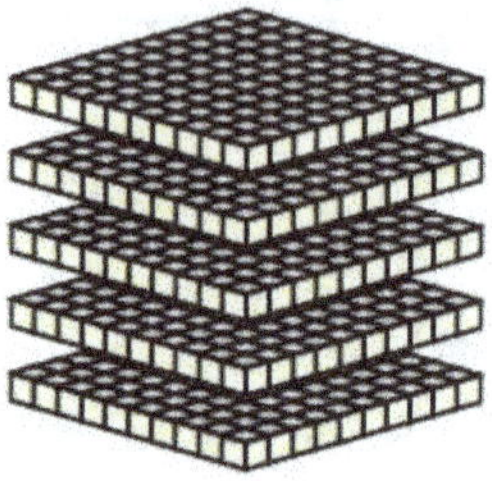
______ Hundreds

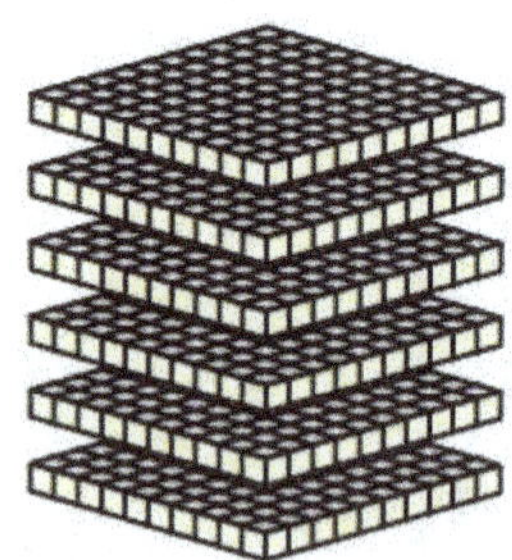

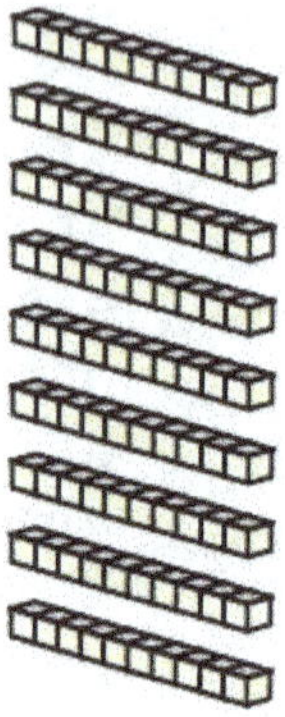
______ Tens

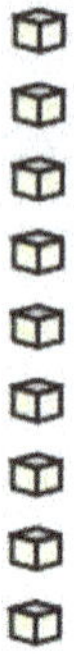
______ Ones

______ Total

2.
______ Hundreds

______ Tens

______ Ones

______ Total

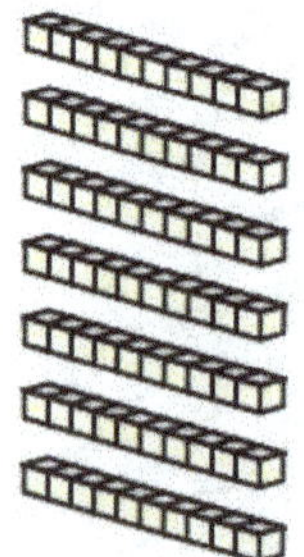

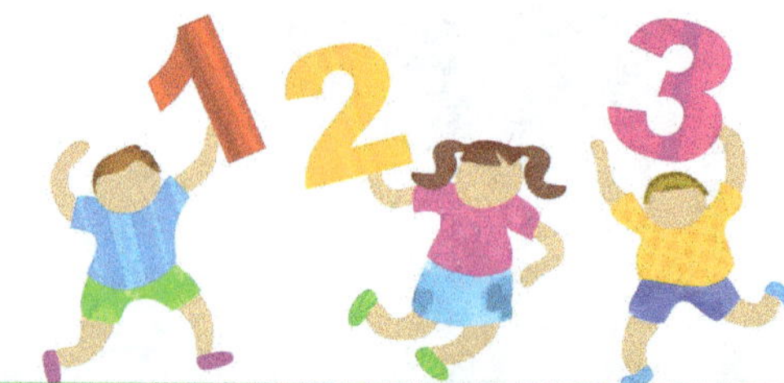

FINDING THE PLACE VALUE

Write your answers on the blank.

1.  __________ Hundreds  __________ Tens  __________ Ones

__________ Total

2. 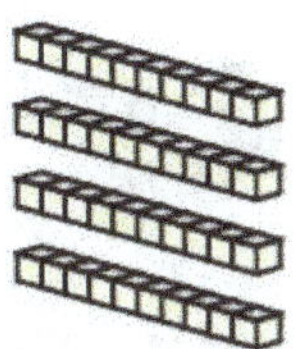 __________ Hundreds __________ Tens __________ Ones

__________ Total

FINDING THE PLACE VALUE

Write your answers on the blank.

1.

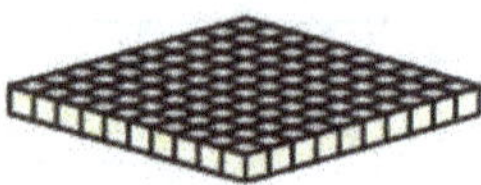 _______ Hundreds   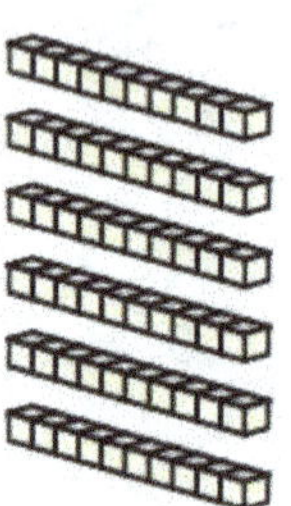 _______ Tens    _______ Ones

_______ Total

2.

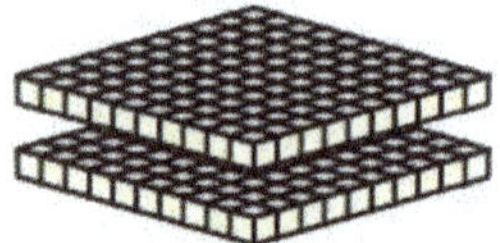 _______ Hundreds    _______ Tens    _______ Ones

_______ Total

GOOD JOB!

ANSWERS

BUILD A 2-DIGITS NUMBER FROM THE PARTS

Write the 2 digit numbers.

1. __52__ 50 + 2

2. __73__ 70 + 3

3. __65__ 60 + 5

4. __70__ 70 + 0

5. __74__ 70 + 4

6. __73__ 70 + 3

7. __37__ 30 + 7

BUILD A 2-DIGITS NUMBER FROM THE PARTS

Write the 2 digit numbers.

1. __66__ 60 + 6

2. __35__ 30 + 5

3. __90__ 90 + 0

4. __14__ 10 + 4

5. __93__ 90 + 3

6. __42__ 40 + 2

7. __60__ 60 + 0

BUILD A 2-DIGITS NUMBER FROM THE PARTS

Write the 2 digit numbers.

1. __13__   10 + 3
2. __21__   20 + 1
3. __57__   50 + 7
4. __53__   50 + 3
5. __89__   80 + 9
6. __76__   70 + 6
7. __29__   20 + 9

BUILD A 2-DIGITS NUMBER FROM THE PARTS

Write the 2 digit numbers.

1. __34__   30 + 4
2. __45__   40 + 5
3. __24__   20 + 4
4. __18__   10 + 8
5. __16__   10 + 6
6. __65__   60 + 5
7. __56__   50 + 6

Write the 2 digit numbers.

1. _____74_____   70 + 4
2. _____90_____   90 + 0
3. _____32_____   30 + 2
4. _____47_____   40 + 7
5. _____56_____   50 + 6
6. _____54_____   50 + 4
7. _____84_____   80 + 4

Write the 2 digit numbers.

1. _____48_____   40 + 8
2. _____71_____   70 + 1
3. _____41_____   40 + 1
4. _____61_____   60 + 1
5. _____53_____   50 + 3
6. _____38_____   30 + 8
7. _____96_____   90 + 6

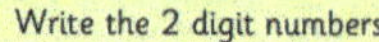

BUILD A 2-DIGITS NUMBER FROM THE PARTS

Write the 2 digit numbers.

1. _____22_____   20 + 2

2. _____86_____   80 + 6

3. _____83_____   80 + 3

4. _____29_____   20 + 9

5. _____20_____   20 + 0

6. _____41_____   40 + 1

7. _____42_____   40 + 2

BUILD A 2-DIGITS NUMBER FROM THE PARTS

Write the 2 digit numbers.

1. _____82_____   80 + 2

2. _____21_____   20 + 1

3. _____71_____   70 + 1

4. _____11_____   10 + 1

5. _____20_____   20 + 0

6. _____70_____   70 + 0

7. _____77_____   70 + 7

BUILD A 2-DIGITS NUMBER FROM THE PARTS

Write the 2 digit numbers.

1. __35__   30 + 5
2. __55__   50 + 5
3. __44__   40 + 4
4. __53__   50 + 3
5. __47__   40 + 7
6. __85__   80 + 5
7. __83__   80 + 3

BUILD A 2-DIGITS NUMBER FROM THE PARTS

Write the 2 digit numbers.

1. __16__   10 + 6
2. __32__   30 + 2
3. __47__   40 + 7
4. __75__   70 + 5
5. __16__   10 + 6
6. __46__   40 + 6
7. __75__   70 + 5

Write the 3 digit numbers.

1. __751__   700 + 50 + 1

2. __947__   900 + 40 + 7

3. __349__   300 + 40 + 9

4. __465__   400 + 60 + 5

5. __585__   500 + 80 + 5

6. __821__   800 + 20 + 1

7. __310__   300 + 10 + 0

Write the 3 digit numbers.

1. __583__   500 + 80 + 3

2. __336__   300 + 30 + 6

3. __287__   200 + 80 + 7

4. __265__   200 + 60 + 5

5. __570__   500 + 70 + 0

6. __459__   400 + 50 + 9

7. __711__   700 + 10 + 1

BUILD A 3-DIGITS NUMBER FROM THE PARTS

Write the 3 digit numbers.

1. __443__   400 + 40 + 3

2. __171__   100 + 70 + 1

3. __984__   900 + 80 + 4

4. __292__   200 + 90 + 2

5. __690__   600 + 90 + 0

6. __352__   300 + 50 + 2

7. __785__   700 + 80 + 5

BUILD A 3-DIGITS NUMBER FROM THE PARTS

Write the 3 digit numbers.

1. __574__   500 + 70 + 4

2. __661__   600 + 60 + 1

3. __676__   600 + 70 + 6

4. __653__   600 + 50 + 3

5. __365__   300 + 60 + 5

6. __984__   900 + 80 + 4

7. __939__   900 + 30 + 9

BUILD A 3-DIGITS NUMBER FROM THE PARTS

ACTIVITY NO. 15

Write the 3 digit numbers.

1. __542__   500 + 40 + 2

2. __864__   800 + 60 + 4

3. __821__   800 + 20 + 1

4. __510__   500 + 10 + 0

5. __681__   600 + 80 + 1

6. __554__   500 + 50 + 4

7. __114__   100 + 10 + 4

BUILD A 3-DIGITS NUMBER FROM THE PARTS

ACTIVITY NO. 16

Write the 3 digit numbers.

1. __291__   200 + 90 + 1

2. __713__   700 + 10 + 3

3. __965__   900 + 60 + 5

4. __554__   500 + 50 + 4

5. __926__   900 + 20 + 6

6. __236__   200 + 30 + 6

7. __860__   800 + 60 + 0

Write the 3 digit numbers.

1. __884__ 800 + 80 + 4

2. __271__ 200 + 70 + 1

3. __738__ 700 + 30 + 8

4. __590__ 500 + 90 + 0

5. __270__ 200 + 70 + 0

6. __443__ 400 + 40 + 3

7. __129__ 100 + 20 + 9

Write the 3 digit numbers.

1. __681__ 600 + 80 + 1

2. __946__ 900 + 40 + 6

3. __469__ 400 + 60 + 9

4. __713__ 700 + 10 + 3

5. __222__ 200 + 20 + 2

6. __666__ 600 + 60 + 6

7. __921__ 900 + 20 + 1

Write the 3 digit numbers.

1. __412__   400 + 10 + 2

2. __272__   200 + 70 + 2

3. __417__   400 + 10 + 7

4. __540__   500 + 40 + 0

5. __657__   600 + 50 + 7

6. __599__   500 + 90 + 9

7. __124__   100 + 20 + 4

Write the 3 digit numbers.

1. __644__   600 + 40 + 4

2. __471__   400 + 70 + 1

3. __477__   400 + 70 + 7

4. __399__   300 + 90 + 9

5. __425__   400 + 20 + 5

6. __162__   100 + 60 + 2

7. __544__   500 + 40 + 4

ACTIVITY 1

1. <u>819</u>

2. <u>945</u>

ACTIVITY 2

1. <u>233</u>

2. <u>654</u>

ACTIVITY 3

1. <u>545</u>

2. <u>986</u>

ACTIVITY 4

1. <u>259</u>
2. <u>477</u>

ACTIVITY 5

1. <u>565</u>
2. <u>221</u>

ACTIVITY 6

1. <u>676</u>
2. <u>737</u>

ACTIVITY 7

1. ____394____

2. ____282____

ACTIVITY 8

1. ____573____

2. ____155____

ACTIVITY 9

1. ____362____

2. ____724____

ACTIVITY 10

1. _____835_____

2. _____487_____

ACTIVITY 11

1. _____736_____

2. _____114_____

ACTIVITY 12

1. _____499_____

2. _____987_____

ACTIVITY 13

1. <u>599</u>

2. <u>671</u>

ACTIVITY 14

1. <u>916</u>

2. <u>444</u>

ACTIVITY 15

1. <u>162</u>

2. <u>226</u>

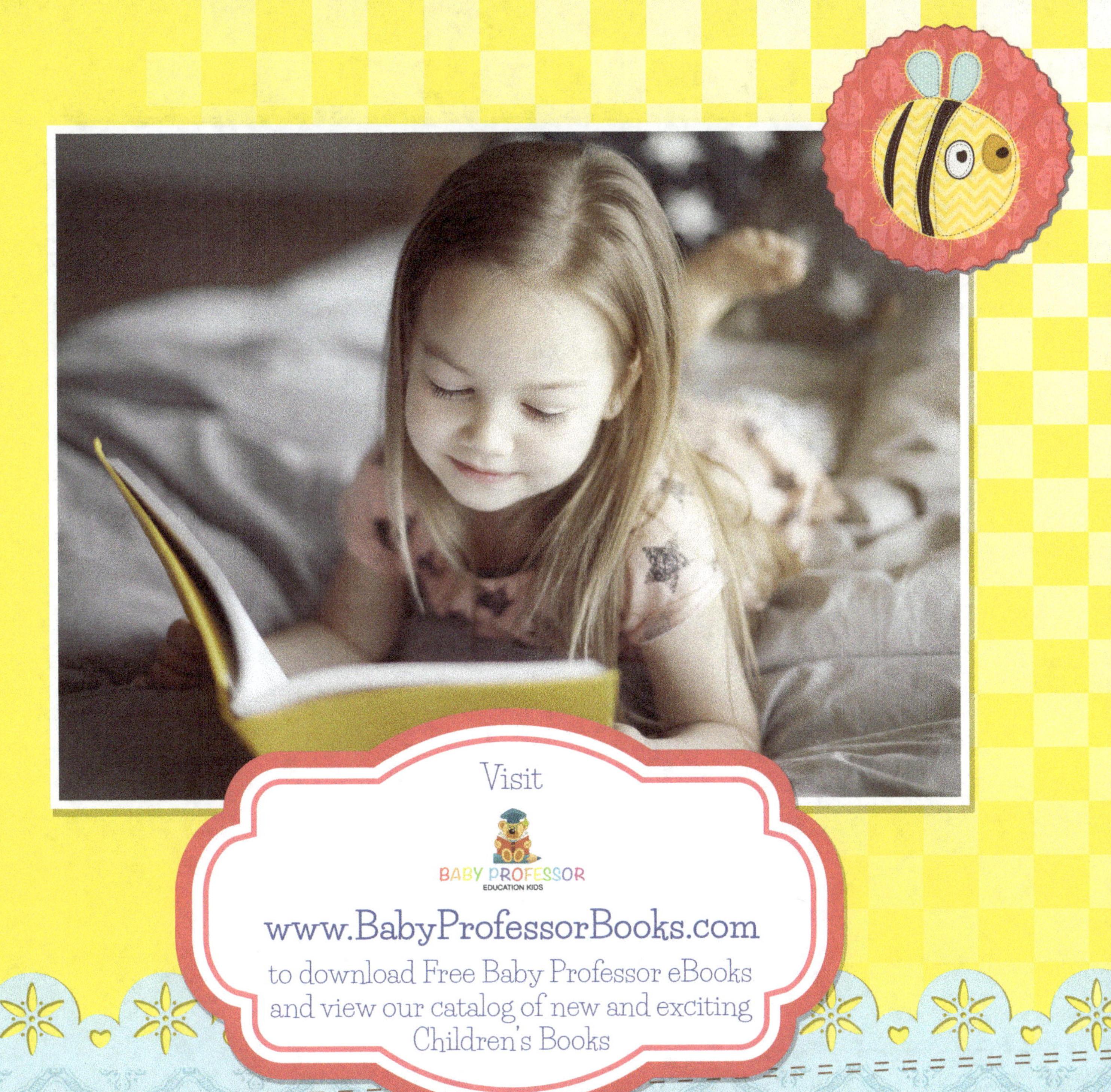
Visit
BABY PROFESSOR
EDUCATION KIDS
www.BabyProfessorBooks.com
to download Free Baby Professor eBooks
and view our catalog of new and exciting
Children's Books